VISUAL
REVELATIONS

RUDOLPH THURMAN JR.

This is a collection of poems that are fiction and nonfiction

Expression of art, views and life and spiritual wisdom from

The authors point of view

Copyright © 2022 *Rudolph Thurman Jr*

All rights reserved. No part of this book may be reproduced or used in any manner without written permission of the copyright owner except for the use of quotations in a book review.

First paperback edition January 2022

Book design by *Natalia Junqueira*

ISBN 978-0-578-32471-5 (paperback)

Published by *IngramSpark*.

Contents

Chapter 1 1

Chapter 2 11

Chapter 3 21

Chapter 4 29

Chapter 5 38

Chapter 6 44

Chapter 1

Resurgence

His soul was searching for a resurgence as he walked into a service he was hurting with his hands up broken with tears in his eyes flowing wanting to bury the pain yearning for a change he knew what he was feeling could no longer remain searching for a purpose constantly reminded of his wrongs wondering if mercy is even deserving not understanding the values of life feeling worthless. Struggling to find his gift surrounded by curses his spirit needs nurturing his experiences is calling for a conversion he stands at the altar wanting a fresh start rinse me create in me a new heart show me the light because all I see is dark I need a spiritual walk the devil is on me like a hawk setting traps blocking me so I can turn back I want the old me gone take my hand so I can walk strong and remain on track place me in a environment that's inspiring. Lay your hands on me and tell me that you're not finished. There's too many people who want me to be diminished. I know much is required to whom it is given but I've fallen many times but now I have risen. This is my resurgence. I'm ready to start living.

Prosperity

I've been patient waiting on my placement understanding my tribulations I'm faced with is only to strengthen me to be amazing my walk brought me clarity covered by spirituality I've been touched by heavenly arms I've had setbacks but now I have been pushed forward and my prosperity now shines as I rise blessings released and my palms are open for my increase poured out continuously taking me to a place of humbleness and grace now I feel safe content with my growth I reached a elevated place. This feels more than a phase God shines on me. I'm covered in a glaze. I'm amazed as I slowly say hallelujah I'm raising up the highest praise grateful for where I'm placed you can see grace in my face. My cup runneth over. I'm receiving more than a taste. It's a blessing to witness the light shining from above. I feel the aura of love I'm in a frame of photosynthesis. My transformation is God's plan. It's inevitable for me to change.

Testimony

Sitting in my conviction trying to understand my position and what is the condition, what is this a sickness I'm conflicted my brain is doing long division walking in the direction of ignorance my vision is tinted. Wishing I had more wisdom for major decisions now consequences is something to live with moving too fast can leave you long winded. I feel like everything that was in my store house has been evicted who do I blame when signs were given the answers were there before the questions but it was ignored along with suggestions I don't want to digest this I can't suppress it I remain calm and rested as I count my blessings thinking of how many times I've been tested and what exactly am I benefiting from what I have invested my testimony will be long a message the truth that lies within in my chest has rested now I project it and break up this congestion I ask the lord for forgiveness for my confessions as he scans through my transgression will I learn through my lessons as I seek direction activating the power within as I begin to start manifesting with tears in my eyes hoping he hears my message. Your child has fallen many times and I'm just so thankful that your arms were there to catch him.

Soul Scripture

I have a gift through my vision messages are given I kill my flesh so my spirit begins living I speak through my writtens flowing with rhythm I form crowds like a playground filled with children and leave my signature wherever I visit the key is for the mind to be free my wisdom will release you from prison my thoughts are exquisite expressing myself eloquently verbal celibacy don't touch my vocabulary I'm a wordsmith forget chills l feel it in my capillaries father forgive them for they don't know what they do oh that's a message for my adversaries. I'm protected by the blood from above. This is love. His home is heavenly. I let his hymns rest in me. I'm guided through his melody, some read palms I read psalms, words of assurance, spiritual endurance cleansing myself as I prepare my cup for more pouring.

Confirmation

When it dropped in my spirit I knew it was mine every word I heard in my mind that told me I was denied was truly a lie my patience has been exercised and I know at times I was denied but there was always a reason why. You see, what's being prepared for us is not something that's always going to be visible to our eyes. Respect the process and position yourself to stay in line. Everything has it's time. The enemy won't have the same vision as mine. His ways I really despise see I know the feeling inside my heart when faith is combined the moment is divine I saw the sign that gave me the understanding on what I couldn't define. I've been in the darkest places and still been able to shine. I can say that I had times when things were right in front of my eyes that I was not able to recognize but I had to elevate my mind to see the disguise. Sometimes the truth is really a surprise I know what may be dead to some God will show you he's not done and that he is still alive my purpose will be aligned. He spoke to me and his voice told me to rise.

Mercy

Conversations with the Holy Ghost oh mercy mercy me father hold me close I feel like I'm drifting I'm going in to a comatose bring me back lay your hands on me bring the feeling back is that healing yes I needed that the truth is what I'm yearning for yes you will reveal the facts show me the way I still believe in better days I'm staring in the sky feeling your rays passing through the shade taking in your sunshine lay your hand on my head make your son wise clear my path and remove the lies things it what it used to be sometimes I'm not even used to me I'm speaking truthfully but I know it's just a part of my growth and your moving me I have questions on the way your using me. When your spirit hits yeah it soothes me life is such a mystery only if we knew everything we're supposed to see no matter what's going on I know you'll cover me Your the greatest nothing will ever replace your love for me. Everyday that you awaken me is validation that there's more for me I've been getting back in to your word lately and I know that you have never left nor forsaken me I know the Devil is chasing me but I'm a fighter and I can't let him take from me he tried breaking me but I know you prepared a place for my enemies. You been great to me in a world where I know there's love but sometimes hatred is so clear to see surround me make it safe for me your presence is a gift to me life is the best thing that you've given me I want to live it abundantly until you come for me but in the meanwhile comfort me I can admit sometimes I feel like you want to see more come from me and all it takes is the faith of a mustard seed your the author and finisher and the director that watches over me from above working and setting up for me from behind the scenes. Please remove the vail from my eyes that's been there so that I can see.

Spirit

I've seen the spirit override whatever comes to mind. Change the direction and correct steps and shift the time. The calendar the father holds is not the same as mine. The moves and the decisions I strive to take is through provision there's a word that is written that's powerful enough to move your position when you're convicted. I'm a fiend and I don't want to crack my addiction I feel it moving through my body healing the sickness I close my eyes and let my head rise requesting more prescriptions I don't just feel high I am lifted wrapped up in his presence I'm gifted this feeling that I have does more than make my body chill I elevate to levels where my flesh is killed tap in to a place where I'm fulfilled learning the will with my eyes to hills the world can strip me but can never give me what the father will that's the Necessity's I love how it flows like seven seas its moving through my body its cleansing me rinse the toxicities.

Discipleship

We are walking testimonies so there's nothing that can be told to us through all the tests and stories the spirit separates all the fake and phony. There's no way to clone thee there's only one that's above so I'm not impressed with anything else that one tries to show me. I don't talk to rocks. I talk to the creator of rocks, forget your clocks my father will make your time stop. All of you devil's your flesh is too hot. My God is in charge shifting me continuously to new spots. I'm a disciple. His word is my rifle I'm strapped with scriptures no vest can protect you the lord is my refuge for every time I fell, he was there to rescue. I had divine moments but I was a mess too. What do you do when words convict you? What direction should you look to rinse you and create in you a new heart a fresh start and looking yourself in the mirror and getting introduced to the new you.

F.O.O.D (FATHER.OPEN.OUR.DOORS)

Father open our doors like the pores on our skin cleanse us refresh us from our sins the daily bread that I digest let it be nourishing and revive us give us something fresh to strengthen inside us in the beginning there was fruit that was given that was forbidden we were always faced with decisions it was written I pray to stay away from positions that would cause me to want more than what is given as I wait on the fruits of my labor I ask you to give me the spirit to not steal from my neighborhood I practice obedience trusting in your ingredients your hands are heavenly I love how you're blessing me with your recipes I know you won't keep your children starving your the farmer of my garden and your seeds will reap from the harvest. When my cup runneth over I feel the strongest my table is prepared with enough to share all I need is provided through prayer I break my fast at dinner discipline strengthens the inner patience is fulfilling when you understand who's the giver.

Sermon

Poetic architecture cut from a different cloth and texture uniquely sculptured in this culture eyes wide open scanning the vultures that's creating illusions to break the focus cleans the mind with mental soaking doors locks until I receive my keys I walk with faith every step I take and breathe and believe I have the strength to break a curse I live and observe my heart carries a word practicing patience destined for greatness thankful and understanding what grace is giving my services to things that's worth it avoiding the serpents moving in silence spiritually guided all I need will be provided and prepared I inhale and exhale fresh air blocking the toxins in the atmosphere you have no access here I don't practice fear negative words fly by no reaction here I'm proactive yeah I move in a motion that's similar to waves in a ocean stroking through the emotions taking notes as my mind sails like a boat to the shore striving to stay afloat. I want more. These hands are deep in the sands. I'm on a surface determined to walk with purpose. The temperature is rising. I'm avoiding the furnace my spirit is discerning. I'm learning what to be distant from as I walk with the son of man, giving him my service this is my sermon.

Chapter 2

Internal Truths

Sometimes my emotions take over and start to speak. The tears fall slowly down my cheek and onto the loose leaf as it becomes the outline to my speech. My eyes hold the truth which will be revealed when the actions appear to be concealed. My words are deep, meant to seep inside the hearts of the strong and weak. I can only give you me and hope that who I show you is what your eyes can truly see. I can't fulfill all the expectations that some may seek, life is time and balance, decisions, choices and challenges, lessons and accomplishments. Some things are damaging. Mysteries twist and turns, what's the time limit for us to learn? how much are we losing, how much will we earn, do we understand value and what do we deserve. Sometimes I just observe. My thoughts are preserved I try to find the right timing to release my words sometimes we want to search for reasons then we hear God's voice speaking telling us to just leave it I know it doesn't feel good when we cant see it but sometimes we don't see that it reached its completion no warning out of nowhere things can be deleted if we are getting redirected we must remain still he sees all things that must be fulfilled a straight path is being created for you so you don't walk down hill. So when you reach where you supposed you to then the reason will be revealed.

Incarcerated Thoughts

I'm sitting in this prison composing this written gripping the bars I'm torn apart heavy on my heart how did I let myself get in to this position my anger I really wished I would have been able to restrict it Now look at me sitting in this cell feeling like hell no chance for bail my actions I can't retract them I snapped and saw blackness all my dreams thrown away because I couldn't walk away blood on my palms from bearing my arms pushed to a point of no return why couldn't I hear the alarm voices screaming in my head no don't do it too late the bullets are released the victim met their fate. An argument gone wrong that didn't have to escalate. It's evil how we can let our egos pull us away from our people. I'm staring at that man as he has difficulty breathing the look he gave me as his soul was slowly leaving, my eyes couldn't believe it. I just killed my brother not the child from my mother but my brother like I just killed someone my color I dropped ashamed of my actions thinking why when I walked away to go to the car I should have just drove away but my adrenaline was too high and it drove me to rage now I'm in a cage with no chance to see the light of day. I never thought I would see the day that I would be one of those black men that took their own away. If I could change the narrative of this story this whole chapter would be thrown away.

Struggles

I've been struggling with these uncontrolled substances having mental rumblings I heard that life is worth living but I think the world would be fine if I wasn't in it I'm leaving nothing behind I have no children who cares about my history or my lineage forget this place I'm staring in the mirror ready to contemplate with this .38 I don't see life in my face these voices in my head won't let me concentrate. I'm sipping this liquor going through my phone staring at pictures. Thinking of times when things were fine now suicide is on my mind I can't lie some things I've been through has me traumatized. I'm doing things that's not myself denying any form of help. Crying on a daily sometimes I scare me yelling out but nobody hears me I'm feeling down and weary in a world that's so cold I'm all alone I haven't heard or felt the word love in so long so how do I hold on when I'm about to fall I'm not strong I'm so gone no one understands me they say I'm so wrong the tune I sing is a sad song my adrenaline is rushing I'm heating up I can't keep calm I pushed everyone away there's no one to call I don't want no sympathy at all this is me I say goodbye with tears in my eyes Pulled the trigger 3 times I'm still alive 2 bullets in the chamber is it not my time or is purpose the reason that I survived I think it's time to find out why.

The Art of Mind

Are we divided by the art or we divided by the heart distractions can have you walking in the dark preoccupied by analyzing lines the sand in the hour glass is passing you by how are you using the time overthinking can have you sinking who are you giving all this power to training people to derail you falling for the traps your being studied on how you react you losing it come back understand that it's only the ones that's on track that's getting attacked can't you see or is it cloudy like cataracts focus on the craft instead of the stats whatever you wrestling with maneuver break the hold instead of tapping out on the mat there's enough room for all, the universe holds many stars but when we don't get what we want we hide behind bars some barriers are reflecting scars new acronym what's really happening does it hurt when you give your all did you not like the reception what about the content and your message should that override the applause. If so analyze the purpose along with your cause and before you start to create take a second and pause what's your format be thankful and know that your welcome but not a doormat who gave you your gift I hope you know that it's the one who oversees us all don't be puzzled he's the only one that can put your pieces together like a jigsaw when your troubled.

Visiting Hours

Tears in my eyes as I walk to the elevator it's killing me inside seeing you hooked up to this ventilator I don't care what they say nothing will stop my prayers I'm giving my all trying to look past the naysayers I'm a believer but I am weak I'm searching for the strength in me the doctors are rushing in the room asking me to leave they have to run some test but I know better than the rest your whole life you being running through test all this pain in your heart and pressure on your chest I'm sorry if I sound selfish by not wanting you to rest I just knew about your plans but we never really know how much time we have because the hours are measured from the heavens with his hands. I continue to stare at your eyelids praying that they would open I'm so broken but I know there's a reward bigger than what this earth can offer eternal life is the real token your spirit will live forever I just felt a unusual breeze oh it must be your time to leave my hands is squeezed then released from holding, visiting hours are now coming to a closing.

Revelation

You knew exactly what position to play and when to speak when to reach how to seek you studied my speech learned my strengths so you can time when to leap in my direction when I was weak standing close enough to see when I move my feet You knew how much to give and how much to keep opened me up so you can dig deep very swift when you creep your ways are mystique you must be waiting for my fall hoping its steep well you been taking notes so have I the truth is in my sheets the table has been set but I've been watching my steps and there's nothing here for me to eat. You're messy. I chose to be neat. There's things that you weren't able to see like whose covering me I switched locations once I felt the sensation I knew who you were but you kept appearing with different faces but I learned things will be revealed to you if you listen closely and practice patience so when I looked in your eye I saw the lies I learned your words and captured your cadence I seen all I needed to see I was studying you knowing that you were studying me be careful of those who try to enter your house with no key the audacity bringing in the dirt and not wiping your feet if there is one thing I learn from a revelation it is to maintain enough wisdom to not put a person back in position so they can repeat.

Observations

I won't be blindsided by the things that happens on the sideline I'm guided, covered, what I need is provided each moment is documented I don't know if you notice that you don't have enough strength to break my focus time is very critical wasting energy to respond to things that don't spark the mind would be pitiful on my list it's less than minimal sharpen up my visuals I just see the typical repetitive, competitive, subjective stuff people be given you I'm not amused not moved nothing consumed some smiles nowadays is formed to confuse I keep hearing the same song I turn the knob to switch the tune. Every time I'm looking for happy days you want to sing the blues, let the sun shine. Why are you trying to change the mood? Look at this black cloud always trying to surround the moon. My spirit is calm but please don't get confused. Composure would never mean I'm a fool. I have a purpose so I know when it's worth it to move, life is about choices so one must think before they choose. Standing in the same spot opens you up to constantly being abused. A Lot of outspoken people are now feeling subdued. Some eyes that are opened are not understanding what they have viewed. Maybe that explains why a lot of us are so confused. No instructions can sometimes lead to self destruction. Responsibility,Accountability will always fall on you. We are all here for a reason and that's to learn something.

Visual Thoughts

The Body language is not matching the words that are being projected images are being conflicted by a person true reflection distractions are put into place to block out the attention. Is the love really there? Too many hugs are done with a lot of tension and too many questions being asked with the wrong intentions. Communication is lost while there's been a rise of misconceptions I'm seeing things different I stare in to dimensions there's so much revelation in the eyes so now it makes sense when you converse with some it's easy to see the lie some people they rotate their head and move side to side because that direct contact makes things hard to hide but I concentrate while some try to contemplate ways to get what they want they study you to see if your gonna grab the bate some people know what your hungry for so all they have to do is decorate the steak set the table knowing your gonna take the plate. Everything has a price, illusions are for sale with a 50% rebate where's the patience we want everything now not knowing there's reasons why we are told to wait. Sometimes we have to turn the other cheek, be discreet and control our face there's a lot of bitter people who can't prosper because they won't let go of hate. Don't think that I can't read you, you may be fully clothed but you see through. The spirit is the password to evil. Isn't it funny the word says we are created equal so I ask we are beneath who the times we live in are critical but I will remain a thinker and continue to be visual.

Lost Souls

Do you know where you're going walking in a direction broken while your souls frozen there's a unidentified person hurting trying to fulfill a purpose yearning to have attachment to things lacking what their worth is unsatisfied and can never find who you are inside self battling the mirror is where you face the most challenges blind to the things that are damaging running away from interactions going in circles got you boxed in trying to shape yourself but falling apart losing your heart and can't pace yourself are you trying to find a place for help. You feel trapped and unaware how you got here. The sounds that are around you are affecting your ears. Are you listening to the atmosphere? The biggest question is where do you go from here?

Disarmed

There's a lot of evil around I can detect it but I feel God's covering when I walk so I know I'm protected his loving is infinite the discerning spirit that I have is listening but I'm prayed up not concerned with whoever anyone calls upon keep your crystal balls, voodoo dolls and all your gimmicks that you use in the dark it don't make sense you think I'm afraid of some incense that's a joke, I'll blow out your smoke where's your heart jealousy and envy only produces bad result that's your downfall mirror, mirror on the wall the reflection is what your battling who do you serve because my lord is the ruler of all I have the vision to see the things that are hidden I won't hesitate to dissect a snake remove your horns secret agendas are being formed smiles from pretendas asking questions with bad intentions like I'm not paying attention the right presence will break all the tension. My spirit is on guard prepared for the war I have stripes and scars I'm on the battlefield like a navy seal there's peace in my soul don't press the alarm I'm still, I'm calm, wise and armed there's not enough of you that can be formed for me to be harmed I'm suited up in the right uniform go ahead bear your arms open your palms cover your face when you yawn I know you're tired, so retire you can't function because your power is not strong, you're gonna be shocked I'm a live wire you just be disarmed.

Chapter 3

DNA

Who am I stare at my tone whats my origin my background where is my home I walk alone my complexion is a reflection of my descendants my history of my people needs to be comprehended we were traded on slave ships names given to us our bodies bare the scars from chains and whips we sing negro spirituals praying for things to shift waiting on a miracle I close my eyes and have visuals of breaking free from this land of taking orders from the man teardrops for my sisters who screamed stop from being held down penetrated on top rights being taking constant violations we faced with many years of hatred feel our pain how can you remove these stains our strength remains as we search for better days looking for a pathway to get away I hear shots as my brother body drops passing by trees breathing a lot another body is hanged up top my race been in a race look closer there's a story in my face our whole lives we been trying to survive the black man and the black woman needs to be revived.

Brothers

How long are we gonna suffer we are too divided we are colliding we need reviving when are we going to start realizing egos are the reason as to why we are dying we should be trying but things are twisted between you and I. I feel we should be unified but there is always a fight between you and I look I'm speaking to you eye to eye that's where we collide your stuck at the low point when I see that we can rise you we keep taking the strength away from one another I'm tired of seeing my brothers kill each other if we converse maybe we can see the hurt the dried up tears in the dirt our hearts are on the outskirts open up the doors of dialogue the shell is too hard defensiveness got us ready to react and snap take a step back what do we lack why do we act instead of searching for facts we attack is it that we are in pain and we use multiple acts to cover the tracks maybe I feel that we can be better than that I'm sick of this script why do we keep auditioning for this turn the page learn new ways guide our sons be their rays shine for our daughters be a leader with structure and order be a man before you try to be father this is the hour to demonstrate your power because we been exposing our weaknesses do you understand how deep this is our true strength that's within has been hidden like a secret who's ready to seek this I have something in me that can help somebody I'm going to leak this you want it let's take it higher out of the fire reach us I have a word in me just like the preachers. I'm giving a sermon that better touch those all the way up in the bleachers to all my brother's, let's begin let's be Men I'm pleading we need this.

Code Red

Code Red bloodshed another one dead more flatlines less heartbeats my heart weeps flashing lights in these dark streets where can I go where no one can harm me excuse me I'm trying to find the direction for protection is it a cross street? roll the dice what's the probability on my life something ain't right we keep crapping out strong holds being applied hear the cries of the people tapping out what's the price for air I just wanna breathe I'll be lucky if you see me exhale fear where is my miranda too much propaganda grab the defibrillator what did I do? We'll tell you later 1, 1000 pump my chest. I'm going into cardiac arrest when lives are lost, who do we arrest? You have the right to keep your eyes closed and rest. Why do I deserve this every time I step outside, my system is nervous, the feeling in my body I can't curve it. There's an appetite for destruction, humanity malfunctioning, someone is cooking something, I smell corruption, our insides are erupting, alarms keep going off, we see the smoke but nobody is doing nothing.

True Colors

Turn on your television and tell me what is that you see major hypocrisy how can it be a security breach another case by another race that's privilege people exercising they hate look how they fulfill it that never could have been me shots would have been fired immediately repeatedly all I ever did was march and that was enough to be marked how many times are we gonna see repeated favoritism displayed in history never have I seen these kinds of acts in a presidency moving through a building in dc so easily now I don't know what you think but that's animalistic behavior to me I see comfortability breaking and entering posing in offices taking selfies holding objects like a trophy what was accomplished tell me meanwhile my people pleaded for their lives I can't breathe, help me I see others given extra rights I'm waiting for someone to justify these actions and tell me that this is right what's the consequence for this high level of nonsense what's the statement it's like we in two different worlds I'm looking at all these shock faces tell me this ain't tasteless and classless climbing walls and shattering glasses all I see is jackasses the only thing great here is the the true colors being exposed to the masses.

Crumble

Have you ever been down and out looking all about but don't hear a sound or a shout what is this all about I've been in trouble face in the puddle my soul yearning for a spiritual huddle is anybody there does anybody care I've made myself so available for people entitlement got some feeling like they are more than equal I guess the signs weren't clear I watch people release their tears while i was the ear but there's a lot steps on the ladder if you watch the stares but now because of a difference of a opinion and refusing to be a minion it's like I'm talking to the air i guess this is what i get for being so sincere some responses were too cavalier am I wasting my time or losing my mind how is loyalty defined you tell me why and who was ready to stand in line so how do you feel so comfortable to stand there and lie is it because i refuse to not be stagnant and die i chose to grow and climb you don't love me your not a supporter of mine i was distorted I learned my value and you can't afford it I move with a cause I watched things dissolve once I evolved in a direction where there was more blessings now I see things as a collective there has been opportunities to correct it but now there's no connection I hope you now can get my message.

The Merge

We are living in a generation where the age gap is causing a lot of separation. We should be merging, building bridges and elevating and strengthening our communication. Understanding each other and extending our hands to one another. Learning has no limits. As long as we are living the focus should be with a brighter vision and not pursued if it isn't. Let's eliminate all that's negative and create and be receptive and giving. The times have changed, but let it not be the cause for our minds to not crave. We must train the brain, even if it has been stained so it can avoid the grave. Teach those who lack ways on how to behave and direct them in the right path so they can be saved. Wisdom doesn't come overnight and it takes more than days but lessons can be taught by the knowledge a person chooses to obtain. Different perspectives are going to be projected. We just have to learn to be collective and respect it. Lets focus on the objective. No one wants to feel disregarded or disrespected. A Lot of us are guarded, misunderstood individuals with things in our lives that were never properly corrected. Different ages of hurt, some of our phases were worst but we can walk together and merge and unite let's make it right. I believe this could work. Whether you are an introvert or overt, let's find a middle ground and become one voice in this world with many sounds. The time is now for every man, woman and child. It's important that we sit down and realize we are staring at a cycle that needs to be worked on before it all breaks down.

Cycles

Becoming a parent you see life through a different lens. You think you understand childhood until you see yourself living again watching repeated ways, reacting at an older age forgetting that there was a time where you had to go through that same phase. I observe your growth teaching you what I know as I'm trying to better me I wonder what your learning and how cautious am I to what you see and what you hear how often do I hold you near sometimes your cries reminds me of my tears I was once you hopefully I don't do the things to you that I didn't like how am I shaping your life I hope you understand this is the adult me raising you so I use my experiences to guide you I still want you to get to a place where you can define you hoping you appreciate the years I contribute I'm half the reason your here still trying to adapt to you I want to create a environment of love for you as you look up at me with a stare like please don't disappoint me because my memory can affect me I hear you every day and life is testing me I have two responsibilities to correct you and correct me God help me as I search for the answers striving to survive finding the strength to provide I think of the times when we don't see eye to eye which can be stressful sometimes but don't let that overshadow when we shine I'm just trying to set you up to have a better life than mine. I promise to protect you and I won't break that lie we're growing together. I remember you being as light as a feather now I hold you by my side watching your smile shocked because I can see my own eyes. Hoping you have dreams just like I. I'm going to show you why living is just as important as being alive.

Warning Shots

Do you feel the shots? no these shots right here aren't meant for your skin. These are warning shots to catch the attention of your sin. There's going to be a high price to pay ignorance is spreading what happened to humanity and its ways where are we heading are these signs of Armageddon we're losing a lot when we will get it the direction that we're going has me thinking are we walking beheaded I don't understand the times that we're in did someone reset it these are dangerous grounds we're walking on these floor are not even cemented we falling in the cracks we falling for the traps buttons being pressed just to see how we will all react can't you see we repeating history why do we keep falling for all of that we keep getting chased by our past I seen this before where's the magnifying glass zoom in society needs a huge improvement every action is deeply rooted the truths in the dirt we point fingers faster than we look at mirrors because the reflection really hurts but maybe we should look at ourselves closely before we look at everyone else first. We hurting each other killing each other could it get any worse look another stretched hearse we out of pocket another family has to empty their purse backs are against the wall let me understand how does this work someone starts a trend and you do whatever to try to fit in eliminate all forms of thinking fall victim to the system the outcome is in two positions your life getting outlined in streets or sacrificed to the prisons.

Chapter 4

Stimulation

I want conversations that's stimulating too much time is being wasted what are we creating when you're speaking there should be purpose in what your saying I'm not cool with being stagnated I long for elevation I get bored because I want more when it comes to intelligence my mind is a open door give me that round table talk that makes the mind walk mental discovery the right surroundings will produce ideas that's astounding certain environments will have your head pounding I can't afford for my mind to be clouded lacking tools in a pool will only result to yourself drowning I need my feet flat on the concrete to feel well grounded I'm no prophet but what does it profit when too much is being invested on topics that's toxic someone outline the logic put me a room with people whose ready to zoom give me wisdom where I can be distant from fools I won't hesitate to shift the way you think we need to elevate what should we eliminate kill the germs let it burn let it fumigate empty talk should never resonate I'm seeing hell and hate how much more we gonna take and what point do we break this is getting heavy its a-lot of weight spark the mind and do the shake your eyes are open but your not awake look around check your space do you feel safe do you feel moved what what was the last thing that really inspire you why you so cool push through the ways that your used to and lets create to a new groove break through this puzzle like Sudoku find the solution to bring the mind to a new room.

Jewels

Ulterior motives mental corrosion's thoughts loaded then projected in multiple directions causing explosions who is it intended for whoever is the closest how do you control this I regain my focus I spot the trickery listen to conversations and decode the mysteries I felt energies that exposed contaminated purities what raises your levels could be a inner battle of insecurities take time to let that set in some titles need revised headings my eyes are on my blessing stay alert on who wants to be apart of your table setting I had a revelation on the preparation how close can you be to someone with no sensation in a room that's consumed if your tuned in to the mood you can feel the separation I'm not moved I scan I zoom I'm no fool I remain cool sharp and smooth and I let you expose you. Time will always show you what it's supposed to. There's a reward in silence. Some people speak too soon, be selective with the words you spew, understand what you hear and know when to adjust the tune every environment is different but some places are hard to get adjusted to. I'm excited by spirits that shake me. I don't want to be able to just move. What you may love some may not be accustomed to but my desire is to be in a place where love doesn't only peek in. I need it to shine right through.

Thoughts

Late night walks and self talks in the park waiting for a spark I gather my thoughts waiting on that moment that ignites my heart taking in the atmosphere my inspiration is in the air I leaped over my fears changed the direction of my year I watched the sunshine so bright it dried my tears now I'm staring at things crystal clear I took a vow with my hand on my chest to speak real sincere listen here as my voice travels through your ears we all have a reason as to why we were put here align yourself to find yourself make a mark before you disappear. How would you define yourself? How much understanding do you have, do you recognize yourself, do you have winning in your vision. Do you have the keys to be driven, does your desires match your given? What fulfills you and what you feel is missing. Are you resilient? Can you display your gifts and be brilliant? Have you set goals? What are you doing to feed your soul? What makes you complete and do you feel whole? Are you satisfied with the life you chose? Are you on the right road if you were to die today, where do you think you're going to go?

Perseverance

I'm guarding my spirit I'm on self preservation with no hesitation I'm not making any reservations with Satan my tongue is discipline for statements temptation be chasing I dwell in the house waiting practicing patience ready for elevation my piece of mind no one can take it The God I serve there's no replacement all the hatred will be annihilated look at my eyes they dilated I was raised with class and greatness everything is timing there's no lateness this is orientation feel the vibration I been lost but found the location Purpose, Passion, Prosperity I was created and given clarity I have a covering that follows me hallowed be thy name I will acknowledge thee I know who I am I'm God's property I say it confidently with Authority I can't be bought and you can not borrow me see the sign caution please I know who walks with me I love life, I love Christ there's no price that can match his sacrifice he's my light con ed couldn't shine as bright as my reflector, my protector, shift my speech language corrector his greatness can't be measured he's the ruler, that's my professor, that I honor the highest scholar the highest power who can move anything even in the darkest hours his clock is on the highest tower my soul is touched with a filled cup he raised me up sheltered me and gave me love been scarred but he healed me up I got a story that's why I give God the glory this voice of mine will shine no matter who ignores me I'm on a journey I could be on a gurney he takes away all the worries your hands are too short to box his flurries is unorthodox he is unlimited so excuse me if I think out of the box my mind isn't created for my thoughts to stop I'm going for the top no matter how many times I drop he moves mountains and I know my rock I pushed through tears I push through fears I fell down steps and climbed up stairs through the years I vowed to persevere dodged situations that could have been too severe but now it is clear to raise my hands up in the air and give thanks, that I am still here.

My Reflection

When the light shines I see who I'm supposed to be. I was hidden in the shadows waiting to see the true reflection of me. The dark covered my heart, as I waited patiently to shine. Was I delayed? Some may say everything happens on its own time. I began to rise with a look in my eyes. I saw the color beaming from the sky that gave me direction, that's when I recognized the dawn of my reflection.

Purpose

I've been properly placed in position to pursue my purpose recognized my value and what my worth is I use alone time for spiritual conversing and form my own personal service there was a revealing to myself on what's deserving things taken out of my life that was a disservice I'm in alignment with my assignment I won't be left behind when its my time for refinement my mind is being shaped for whatever enters so I can define it wisdom and vision I will combine it understanding my walk changing my talk exercising the words trusting in what I project learning how to reject being in circles where I can connect practicing patience and respect sparking topics of intellect displaying introspects having ideas move me when I haven't even shifted yet. Information flowing that hasn't fully moved through some systems yet some steps that you set is going to have to be taken with no regrets when time is vital they won't be moments of resets no recess a lot of lessons without a thesis if something is for you it don't matter who it is a stranger could be used to reach us don't just look at the features we can miss the blessing judging the dressing and will never understand why we keep missing the message.

Destiny

My mind is crafting I'm taking action on my passion to succeed knowing that time is not everlasting what's in my heart I must go after it I'm given life so I'm automatically drafted My yesterdays are behind me I moved past it My hunger has risen from my fasting memories move through my mind in flashes All I see is a split screens two views of me Passion driven and a person whose trying to figure out what's next with what I've been given. Life is in constant motion. We must find the rhythm time is ticking widen the vision I reach higher because I know who supplies the provisions through all my loses I can still see that I was designed for winning how many times have the pressure been on as things get thrown at me the bat is gripped for the 9th inning I keep swinging eye on my target I'm bravehearted faith walking spiritually guarded rejuvenated I believe the covering I have is causing me to feel illuminated I learn through lessons every failure pushed me to greatness and nobody can take it my story is written my actions and decisions is the only thing that can cause a revision I will strive to give life the best of me as I walk in to my Destiny.

Visual Literature

Eyes in the scope scanning the lens no need for refocusing I see the picture and understand the print along with the signature the truth is in the lines the revelation is in the scripture I'm delivering visual literature when too many hands are in the pot it can cause a mix up its one thing to watch who pours for you and another to watch the cup you sip from I'm aware how I position my chair for tables that are prepared I see the enemy has steps to their stares I see how this is shaping out a lot circles are really squares I won't be cornered over there I can't be boxed in I know the combination if I ever get locked in I kept doors open but that wasn't enough maybe that's why some windows were broken how fare can you be if you gave all the tokens sometimes we don't notice the silent ones are the most outspoken what happens when you present chances but leave with no answers just glances that's overlooking the circumstances too much tip toeing and tap dancing I guess we all have different perspectives of taking stances should my feet only be planted where the sand is I was thinking I should soak it the temperature is changing around this ocean how deep should I go as far as the boats is I'm stroking and the tide is open

I'm floating I see the waves I'm focused you can try so many ways but my experience makes me able to move through the motions.

Time Linez

False narratives being written by pens of deception too many people walking around who feel like their life is perfected who do you serve who do you go to for your own confessions all these thoughts but no questions some things that enter the mind needs directions to the exit I walk with vision you're about division these calculated ways aren't added up so how do you think we sum up the difference look how many things that are showing that we thought were hidden I see the movements but its lacking a lot of rhythm its off track whats coming out your mouth is forbidden no fruit what are you planted without a root your angle is acute you have all the tools but can't explain why the screws are so loose you turning in the wrong direction and its gonna fall apart right in front of you too many chain of events I'm trying to link it but it doesn't connect but you don't see none of the jewels maybe you feel like if you have enough ice it can cover all of the parts that are bruised but keep covering I guess its keeping you cool how do you teach principles in a class without calling it school there's semesters and theirs seasons its up to you for things to improve there's no one to blame when the time fades it will fall right on you.

CHAPTER 5

Ghostwriter 2

I am the hidden hand orchestrating the plan from the shadows making your pens move and tackling your inner battles let your emotions flow I'm the fire behind the smoke the light that shows you where to go I spark ideas and push barriers and break fears give releases and expose secrets and cause tears produce patterns with distinctive ink and prints stimulating minds if they feel dry and rinsed I'll make you rise and think creating paragraphs is my craft I have a bin of rough drafts stories untold that I won't unfold I go back as far as scrolls I am the mental reminder staring at all the fine print my vision is the magnifier watch how I zoom in on this sounding off the alarm giving you the movement in your arm I've shifted moods so smooth from anger to calm I gave you songs, I brought the feeling back in your palms. produced books, changed images, revised looks with the gift of movie scripts. I told the story of many. My closet is filled with too many manuscripts but go ahead and take a bow in front of the crowd. The response is loud as I bless you while I hold the handkerchief. Shhh, only you and I know whose signature this is.

Word Play

I guess it's time to address you am I running through your veins you should have known I am a vessel we two different people you think we're distant and we are divided by egos close I know we're distant and we are divided because your evil my mind is cerebral you can't fool me I see all the lies you spread to the people the more you take shots I can see your spots don't care how many seeds you plant I can relocate to new plots maybe you thought i would fall for the traps but I'm not running around sorry I can't get stuck there save that for the rats you're hoarding maybe you think I care about all the stuff you're choosing to stack I'm on a journey and nothing is going to way me down on my back everything I need is packed. I'm in alignment. I got drive, I question how you got your license. I see all the reckless stuff you specialize in. You're too messy you think your playing your cards right you think you have a full house but you're missing a uncle Jesse you activate my scanners, raise eyebrows and antennas I don't know what you up but I'm alert to my parameters you're a bad planner fix your posture you have bad table manners you're patiently searching for information wondering when I'm going to discharge I'm anti devil you're Antichrist that's two different levels. I'll apply pressure like the last few seconds on the stop clock. You can't box me if I'm in the circle but at any angle I'll still be able to take a straight shot.

P.I.A.N.O

Passion.Intimacy.Affection.Nurtures.Others

The first time I met you I knew instantly you were the one. It just felt so right. Your distinctive look, 88 layers of black and white I love your style. I couldn't wait to touch you. Your texture is so smooth there's so many keys to choose. I'll position my fingers on any part of you pressing slowly to hear your beautiful sounds release. It amazes me how touching you pleases me these sweet melodies of highs and lows it feels good to play with you slow from the day till night I discover you more I'll use other fingers to hear your chords I hope you are just as pleased as I am I never took any lessons My eyes are closed as I follow with feeling My hearing guides me to the right spots to hear your notes our renditions are not repetitious you give me so many options I'm addicted, challenged but able to manage satisfied by your various vibes how can a organ feel this great inside I love you and I say that with so much pride You're my one and only instrument our connection is so intimate I couldn't think of a better pair we light up the room when we get in to it. The Power you have causes people to start rekindling, your music causes mental drifting creating conditions shifting postures and positions that's so beautiful and uplifting. You got my attention. I'm here to listen.

The Process

Sometimes I take long car rides with no one inside window cracked to feel the breeze views from the highway watching the atmosphere as the birds fly by stare into the sky in the night as the lights on the tall buildings shine in these streets of NY where is it going to take my mind I pull over the ride like there's something inside its just when poetry calls I have to come to the front of the line I can never predict the time that this pen of mine is going to glide but I know the sun doesn't have to be out for me to shine I've been given the gift to write touch the hearts and lift the light I lift my hands to Christ the one who gives me life my source of energy who can shift things to right my vision is right and has been written I walk with authority and precision appreciate the living with a spirit of giving maintaining a positive attitude I can't measure the magnitude unconditional love doesn't come with limits my creator will continue to be working on me until he decides that he is finished.

Unraveled

I've opened doors with open arms and gave people the floor the table been set holding it in only brings pressure to the chest Too many pieces on the board we don't need to play chess free your thoughts conversations are becoming a lost art a lot of feelings are being hidden in the dark I never signed up for any games real adults speak from the heart I don't cut corners or hide behind blocks I see the signs and realize when to go and when to stop The path is clear I'm not stumbling on rocks time is in motion whether are not your watching the clock what we talking about too many mysteries when are we gonna let the truth out you can give people all the directions and they they'll still choose a new route the wise ones know when its feeling strange in the environment its time to move out Its not just the snakes I watch its the sly fox the sheep's who portray to be shepherds a leopard will always shows its spots awkward movements making it hard to interact its bad enough when your face to face you still can't get any eye contact phone calls fading because you didn't realize when people needed you it came with a expiration a lot silence occurred with no explanation you ever wonder how people can walk away with no hesitation I can tell you sometimes things happen in the dark but thank God for revelation.

R.E.A.L. Part 2

I remember that moment that I realized everything ain't love it was that time I recognized that people were trying to keep you blind cloud your vision like cataracts people forgot how to interact it got replaced with subs people will take the the time to express themselves in their stories instead of being honest with you and tell you the true story what is it that I'm missing besides the fact that snakes move different they can be in your peripheral vision not all of them are hissing unfortunately some of us don't find out until we are bitten (ahhhhhh) my arms is dripping just a little jewels but to tell you the truth a lot of relationships lost its connection is it the signal or the carrier we just too far apart that's long distance I'm trying to stay in shape I don't want to be long winded I think we all have different perspectives on giving there seems to be a battle between supporting and distorting how many people ever been around someone that always needed you but now they can't be found but I never reported it I just mentally recorded it because people only need you when it's time to feed you and once they get what they want they longer need you there seems to be a bad case going around of amnesia the temperature is rising it looks like a fever but I can shake it life is really a test I'm just trying to live too many of my people are dying and stressed I use to think that things would change but when things don't register you have to change the lanes if you're trying to clean up something you don't do it by adding more stains I can tell you one thing I don't care about about no secret chats that people form to have words roll off their trap that they can't retract i'm a writer with no writers block I'll block a writer you must be sleeping you got the itis my touch is the Midas you smell me clear your sinus I have a question should there be any men that is jealous of women you kidding that's a kitty cat I said what I said and I won't take it take it back or go tit for tat too much fake stuff going on and I won't stand for that boomerang it's time to bring the real back.

Chapter 6

Reconnected Souls

When our eyes connected something inside resurrected there was silence while our smiles translated the message we couldn't help ourselves from the stare I don't know what it is but i recognize the glare like you we were once here it's like our bodies were trying to remind us when we embraced a familiar soul but a different face how we used to hold each other near we have questions with the hope that the answers will be clear there's something about the way you open up your emotions makes me feel like I once wiped your tears our conversations brings us to a place where I feel like deja vu there is missing pieces to this puzzle of me and you. Is it that I'm given another chance to relearn you the closer we get all these theories begin to feel so true I'm speechless at times when I hold you will time give us a clue? or is our purpose just to start something brand new? We left a mark on each other that we both identified as we scan through when we made love we looked at each other like how could this be the first time we were shocked to how our bodies were being handled the heat we were making was melting the candles if our love is getting a do over we will take it higher than it's ever been and leave no room for it to ever be dismantled because I can't afford to lose you ever again.

Turmoil in the temple

From the outside looking in it will appear that they have it all. The big house, double circle driveway, the flowers look so perfect on the nice cut lawn. Who would ever guess that behind these walls would be people that's so empty they don't have anything at all. Sometimes you can't even hear an echo in the hall. Other days it will sound like everyone inside is at war. A house so divided there's no love at all. We invested in all this space to be distant. All these rooms, all of the lights, dining room and big kitchen. Dining table, mats neatly placed, chairs all in position, and no one ever sits in it. Everything is all decorated just like a disguise to hide the truth that there are major keys missing. Skeletons in the closet that no one wants to revisit. A scarred woman inside that struggles with forgiveness, who took in a child from her husband that was sleeping with women. Meanwhile he's fathering a daughter he taught was his for years because the child looked like him but it isn't. Let's just say she had the wrong idea of family traditions. On top of all of that their first born is dealing with a drug addiction. The stress is at an all time high . These are unhealthy living conditions. It's difficult to recognize this though, through these windows everything is out of control. The hate and disgust that's displayed for each other makes you wonder if they really care for each other. They sleep in separate beds and scratch their heads and try to understand what is happening. No connection, just disrespecting. A home of neglect, with people inside who can't stand mirrors because it shows a ugly reflection. But they maintain a different image outside these doors but who would have guessed it. They're the most beautiful family in the neighborhood. They know how to keep it together outside these walls to look good. She's a nurse and he's a doctor. Look at the irony. Two people in the health field living in sickness, that maintain a life with double depictions. What type of prescription here should be giving this is not a house, this is more of a clinic. A home with no structure will lead to destruction; this needs to be reconstructed with instructions with a new outline and new vision. I just wanted to paint this picture to show you that no matter how it looks on the outside, not everyone that has a house is living.

Shattered

Back and forth bickering nobody is listening disrespectful words are lingering from the bedroom to the kitchen and the kids are afraid looking at the adults very different no control in the home anger has caused a lot of distancing their heads are down because they don't know who to look up to now their behaviors are reflecting the ones whose suppose to show them the way and correct them but who they should be getting guidance from are also the ones who need directions. Scared behind these walls storing information deep stares becomes the primary form of communication anger being taken out at the wrong person missing days of love brings more days of hurting. A full house of neglecting lack of understanding and no connection is starting to feel like danger what happens when a family that's been living together starts to feel like strangers. Who are you this is unrecognizable behavior the bodies don't match the actions what happens when your too tired of uncomfortable interactions. Should you just stay silent or start reacting how many things should be ignored, who's gonna take the initiative and be proactive. All these questions that are building time is waiting for you to ask them but when you get used to patterns sometimes you look right past them but how many things can be avoided we can't always masked them. Is there anyone in here that cares about what's happening. Selfish actions is causing innocent ones to be damaged.

Disconnection

Hello! Are you there? lately it seems like you've been so difficult to reach the conversations are to a minimal I don't feel the same when we speak I remember how we used to love to talk I don't understand how the lines got crossed there was so much to say now every word got short it's like the effort got lost we had priceless talks did we lose our patience now we no longer value the cost was it how we were operating there was a time when all we did was converse from the heart now we can't find the spark our tones changed things it ain't the same it went from the light to the dark we use to have intellectual dialogue now I question are we doing anything for our minds at all ?do you care? Hello! Are you still there? oh you said yeah! All I hear is air. I'm sorry there's just a lot of silence that I would have thought I lost the call. I don't want this to be forced at all. Are we wasting our time? Is any of this being absorbed at all? No one wants to talk and feel like they are wasting their message. It seems helpless. Maybe there was a point where we realized we no longer were being respected but you would think that even if buttons were being pushed they would be some sort of effort to correct it but instead we started to fade away and lost the connection.

Exposure

Time will expose the truth like it's supposed to do the seed was planted might as well show the root everything that was hidden has risen false words begin to diminish everything that you try to polish will have a bad finish when you don't carefully listen things will be hard to distinguished but part of a person's cleansing is for toxins to be extinguished the moves in the dark shows your heart sneakiness has become a art I'm trying to connect the things that's told in parts that covers the deceiver and tears others apart the same evil that has mislead people many has been fooled but as things get removed the ones who have been misconstrued will no longer be confused it amazes me what you can find when you clean a room the dirt will always be attempted to be swept away once you have a broom. Whatever you are holding, ask yourself how long can you store it in a place where you know that what may be closed for now will eventually be open.

Healed

You were never taught how to love there was no direction to affection years later it's reflecting how your being affected it's going to take more than a few seconds for me to dissect this the example you seen should have been corrected what a infection but who was gonna translate the message you can't feel when your in the presence of something real so you over analyze and inspect it you have questions your heart is heavy it never rested its wounded and needs caressing it starts from when were adolescents the things we see and observe the projection of words some visuals can hurt and I can see that l.o.v.e. is not always so visibly things can change even if you been in misery conversations should have happen so you could be at ease some things we lose are hard to retrieve a hug should never be something that you ever have to plea no need to put the blame on yourself and feel guilty it is not your fault the dark can only lead the dark but when the light shines it will ignite your heart your time is coming stop running let me tell you something it's only just begun lift your eyes to the hills prophecy will be fulfilled negative words will be killed what you want must be expressed remove the seal it's time to heal let the emptiness inside be filled. What's to come is the best joy over depressed the hand that's being extended from above is laying right on your chest.

Realization

Honor your mother and father for your days would be long, practice respect and obedience and your ways would be strong, a home supposed to guide you as you age to become who you are. Be thankful for what you have there's many homes that never had anyone to lean on, depend on, cherish the ones we have and don't use the time wrong make moments instead of statements it'll be too late when their gone I've seen many fail to plan and things diminished faded away like sand when the wind hits remorse and convictions sits in a place in your body where you can feel sick where there's no medicine to absorb when you need it. Some situations make you numb but all we need is healing holding grudges and never budging won't open doors you won't even see it I can feel it there's something missing and we need it but when you know it and you make no motions to seek it, it will remain hidden like a secret is there something someone said that struck a chord when too many things are in front us it makes it difficult to move forward missed opportunities focused too much on the scrutiny thinking so hard on who responsibility falls on living a life knowing that no one is always right but feeling your never wrong cutting people off makes it hard when you need someone to call upon. It may be difficult to let bygones be bygones but some chances we don't get then here comes regret when someone says bye and you realize that they're gone.

What is Love?

I'm taking my time before I put together my sentences I want to speak on love but not before I grasp whats written in the book of Corinthians through my studies I learned that love is not to be envious it's not evil we should rejoice in the truth that's right people how I see it we should humble ourselves I'm just a pupil any seeds that I plant it should be fruitful anytime I spend should be useful I don't want to dwell in the presence of where people will use you fool you we shouldn't have to guess if its love mixed movements will confuse you is the love afloat is it failing where is going is it sailing from my understanding it is patient expand the mind how are your ways love is kind open up the eyes there needs to be a wisdom override love is too big to be selfish I can't contain something than is worldwide its beautiful like watching the sunrise embracing the morning breeze or waves in the sea or the colors of the leaves that change on the trees love is beautiful if it's anything else God then its just not for me.

Foundation

From the beginning we put in ground work a union with beautiful benefits love from above orchestrated by the father matrimony created in honor we received a heavenly sponsor ordained and co-ordinated a mate with a soul that can't be duplicated we spent years building learning and fulfilling we offered a love to each other that I can stand firm today and say we were both willing we are each others walls through the cracks and all we have each others backs with enough support if we were to fall to maintain a foundation both must give their all understanding the core and how its built a house becomes a home through layers that's put down I'll walk with you no matter if its on stilts just as long as we know where we are going I pray as we age that we can both say we are growing some experiences will break you while some will reshape you blessings, lessons, corrections guidance from the counselor will give us directions as we live our lives that were given with imperfections enhancing our communication for a better reflection whats on our fingers is just a symbol it starts from the heart your wrapped in my arms let's strive to be in a environment that's warm stare into the sky together and shine with the stars no matter how tough it gets what God put together shall always stand strong.

Dedication Page

First and foremost I would like to thank God. All things are possible because of him. I wanna thank my lovely wife for believing in me and my dreams. To all of my close friends, family and supporters I appreciate you more than you know. I've been blessed to have some amazing people in my life on this journey of creating this second book and to those people I thank you for being who you are to me I love you dearly. To any one else whoever pushed me in anyway I would also like to thank you very much.

www.ingramcontent.com/pod-product-compliance
Lightning Source LLC
Chambersburg PA
CBHW071845290426
44109CB00017B/1924